CO-CREATE
WITH
CONFIDENCE

LEVERAGE
YOUR VOICE
AND
CAPITALIZE
ON YOUR
TALENT!

CHARLENE HARRY

Copyright © 2023 Charlene Harry
Published by Krystal Lee Enterprises (KLE Publishing)
All rights reserved. No parts of this book may be reproduced, distributed, or used in any manner, including photocopying, recording, or other electronic or mechanical methods without the prior written permission of the copywriter owner, except for the use of brief quotations in a book review and certain noncommercial uses permitted by copyright law. To request permission, contact the copyright holder, addressed "Attention: Permission to Reproduce Co-Create with Confidence" at
contact@charleneharry.com

Paperback: 978-1-945066-28-3
Audiobook: 979-8-9879709-2-8
E-book: 979-8-9879709-3-5

Edited by: K. Lee
Photographs by: LeTony W. Hadnot Jr.

First Printing Edition in 2023
7 Steps to Clarity
133 North Friendswood
Suite 175
Friendswood TX 77546
USA
www.successwithcharlene.com

Disclaimers
The information in this book was correct at the time of publication, but the Author does not assume any liability for loss or damage caused by errors or omissions.
These are my memories, from my perspective, and I have tried to represent events as faithfully as possible.

PREFACE

Have you ever got hit in the face with a ball and way too late someone says, "think fast!" Would you agree life can make us feel that way? Life can make us confused, uncertain, and question our clarity. When every question, thought, idea, hope or dream pulls at our attention, we can feel like Medusa with several heads going in too many different directions. If someone were to look in your eyes they would see you are overwhelmed, lost, and looking for clarity. Or maybe it was just me who felt this way once upon a time?

For a long time, I prayed for clarity. I began to recognize that clarity came from my ability to hear a voice. Not just any voice, but "my inner voice" that called me from within. As I grew and developed from a child to an adult, I focused mostly on external voices. Over time, these external voices became the leading voice in my head. When my prayers were answered, it became crystal clear to gain clarity I had to look within and not focus as much on who and what was around me.

I am so excited to share the lessons I have learned and the steps I took to listen to the voice within that gave me clarity and still does. I realized we live in a world that requires a massive amount of our attention and that same world often projects its agenda on us and influences our choices. At this rate, it's inevitable to feel unclear about our voice when other voices are heard more loudly. What you hear on replay and say, you will become and do. Like a parrot, if you keep hearing the same words eventually you will speak them.

In these times, it is critical to know how to get back into alignment with what is right for you. You were created by the Creator of all things to live a good life. Although you were created to live a good life, your life is shaped and impacted by your choices. You can choose to align with the good you've been granted or follow choices that separate you from it. For people who feel overlooked or uncertain about their future, what is certain, you will be with you all the days of your life. You are born and get to decide if you will live being you! If you need clarity on who you are, rediscovering your talents, the dream, and mobilizing your future, I am part of the solution.

There is no coincidence that you are reading these words or that you picked up this book. I am sure you did so because you desire to take steps to get clear about your destiny. Innately, you made a decision to stop trusting man and to start trusting in your true source, your Creator. When you connect with this infinite source, you will begin to master the power of Co-Creating with Confidence. It is my hope and desire that you choose to hear the Creator's Voice within Your Voice.

DEDICATION

This book is dedicated to my loving and supportive husband and to our four beautiful children and their children's children. May you find clarity along your journey in this physical life.

Much love,

~ Charlene Harry

CONTENTS

INTRODUCTION *1*

STEP ONE: CLARITY

CHAPTER 1 .... *5*

Trust Your Inner Desire

CHAPTER 2 .... *19*

Identify Your Story

CHAPTER 3 .... *31*

Self-Talk Is The New Self-Care

CHAPTER 4 .... *43*

Design Your Emotional Rollercoaster

STEP TWO: ACTION

CHAPTER 5 .... *57*

Conscious Clarity And Its Connection To Time

CHAPTER 6 .... *71*

Confidence Connects With Actions

STEP THREE: RESULT

CHAPTER 7 .... *81*

Co-Create With Infinite Intelligence

CHAPTER 8 .... *89*

(Bonus Chapter) Manifest Your Desires Daily

Let's Keep In Touch *93*
Work Cited *99*
Bio *101*
Book Description *103*

Introduction

Are you an overwhelmed, overworked, over-thinker who is just plain *"Over it?"* Are you over feeling unsupported, undervalued, and unconfident in your career and life goals? Maybe you are unsure how to tap into your full leadership potential? Or, do you have a wealth of experience and skills, but struggle to leverage them for financial abundance and overall success? I used to be this woman and for each question I had to raise my guilty hand. If that is you also, you are not alone. Many women today face the same challenges, juggling the demands of work and family while trying to navigate their career paths.

But what if I told you that you already possess God-given talents and abilities to unlock a life of abundance and fulfillment, would you believe me? What if you could gain clarity and confidence in your path, and learn how to leverage your unique strengths and experiences to achieve your desired goals?

As a student learner or working leader or both, I am certain that you face many challenges and obstacles. In the midst of hurdles and adversities, know that you have been gifted with God-given talents that can help you achieve your goals with confidence through my 3 Step CAR Method. The "C" is Clarity of the desired objective to be confident in. "A" is Action towards the objective and "R" is Result signs that get you closer to your desire. This book is a guide to help you discover and own your strengths and talents. I want to help you leverage your voice, energize your plan, and capitalize on your talent. Know that you deserve and were made for so much more. I want to help you dig up what has been buried within you.

We will explore how to obtain clarity and breakaway from distracting voices. I offer you an opportunity to market your talents as a resource to achieve your career objectives, entrepreneurial desires, relationship goals, and spiritual advancement. Life balance is possible and you will begin to see opportunities align with your desires as you gain emotional clarity on your journey. Through the insights, practical advice, and milestones shared in this book, you will learn how to leverage your experiences and transform them into opportunities for wealth. You will gain the confidence to take action toward your goals and create a life of abundance and fulfillment.

Here's the thing: action is the key to building confidence. Actions you practice will stick or form a habit. At the end of each chapter, I have created 5 to 15 minute exercises and a deep dive into milestone actions to support each exercise. These implementation steps are here to help you gain clarity on what you learn about yourself and monitor your time management as you recall the information. Consider this an opportunity to watch for the clues that point to your success.

I am here to celebrate your investment in yourself. As you read and take action you will become conscious of your unique story which will lead to your success. Whether you are just starting out in your profession or looking to take your career to the next level, this book is for you. By the end of this journey, you will have gained the clarity and confidence needed to leverage your God-given talents for an abundance of wealth and success.

So, let's begin this journey toward finding clarity to release your talents, amplify your voice, and pave the way to the fulfillment, abundance, and wealth you deserve.

CHAPTER 1 | Trust Your Inner Desire.

STEP ONE: CLARITY

CHAPTER 1

TRUST YOUR INNER DESIRE.

"My inner-self gets me! She wants nothing but the best for me!"

- Charlene Harry

Childbirth is a miracle. Every child is born with a unique fingerprint that cannot be duplicated. When you witness childbirth for the first time, I'm sure you will feel a connection with the baby on a deep level. I believe this connection is a spiritual connection. You should know, everyone who breathes is a miracle. Before we were clothed with flesh and made blood and bone, we were an idea, a spirit, embodied within the Divine.

As babies develop and grow, they are influenced, impacted, and molded by their learning environment. They develop characteristics and temperaments unique to their DNA and social experiences. The way they see life will be determined by the social and cultural context in which they live and thrive. Miracles are special and exciting at the start, but over time, they can appear to fade from memory. Life tends to do a great job at distracting us and removing our attention on the things we should care about most.

You should regard yourself highly and never forget it. But have you forgotten that you were a born miracle? Have you lost yourself in the shuffle of family tension and conditioning? Think back to being a child, were you able to be comfortable making up your own mind about yourself?

There was a time in my life that I did not trust my inner desires. Furthermore, my ability to trust my own judgment was a challenge. As a child, my sister and I depended on the adults who held the responsibility to choose what was best for us. Although we were raised together, as the saying goes, we are nothing alike. One womb, two miracles with unique talents, born 6 years apart.

I knew early in life that I was destined to do something with my talents. I unconsciously said yes to many things, even to the point that "yes" became my mantra. Do I want to make my parents smile, "yes." Do I feel like teasing my sister, "yes." Should I find a handsome boyfriend, "yes." Is it time for me to get married, "yes." Have children, of course, "yes." I realized it didn't stop there though, "Charlene, should you build your career? "yes." Somewhere inside of me, I knew that my life had meaning. My desires drove me to say "yes" to the above. Little did I know that my talents would slowly reveal themselves to me again.

I am known for my magnetic energy, my illuminating smile, and creative expressions. From a young age, I recognized that communication was my talent. As you take inventory on your talents, I want you to notice how your talents are unique to the way you were created; also, they were present when you were born. When we ask the right questions, the answers on the inside will emerge. Asking questions is the first step on the road to self-awareness. Take a moment right now to ask yourself, "What are my talents?" I'll wait. Do you trust yourself and know what your talents are?

May I tell you a little about me? As a young girl, I knew and trusted my talents without any doubt. As I grew into a woman with more responsibilities, I began to doubt my talents and where to use them. What was within my reach as a child seemed like a distant fantasy when I turned 35. Growing up, acting was my thing! I loved to act and felt that I was built for both the stage and the big screen.

Knowing what I loved never went away, but became less clear on their place in my life as people questioned my gifts because they made me question me. They would ask questions like, *What do you want to be when you grow up? What do you want to have in life?* The desires came and went for me to use my acting skills as I grew older. Then, there came a time when my desire would no longer be ignored and demanded I make room for acting in my life. When your desires come into your heart, take residence, and never leaves, it's a strong indicator to pay close attention. Pay attention because those nudges can give you insight about your talents, purpose, and calling.

What about you? Is there something you used to love to do as a child that faded because you couldn't find a place where it fit in your adult life? Did you like drawing or painting new images that you thought were beautiful? Or, you were talented at singing, dancing, writing, taking things apart and putting them back together?

For some of us we have to think back pretty far to remember a inkling of these we liked as a child. But I want you to try

CHAPTER 1 | Trust Your Inner Desire.

and remember hearing those hard questions that made you second guess the desires in your heart? I wanted to play volleyball as a child but finances and time were not there.

Reflect on your childhood talents and consider what you were drawn to? What were you good at? What felt right? Take the time you need and then think about the experiences that point out your talents. List the experiences briefly below that reveal what you are naturally good at. If you are still not sure what to write, consider what people say you liked as a child. Think about their stories of you and see if any of it pulls at your memory. Now, write down what they said you were known for? _____

_____

_____

_____

_____

_____

Now that you have listed the evidence that supports your talents, take a moment to reflect on what you really want in life? What imprint do you want to leave? What will be your legacy? What do you want to be remembered by? What do you want the dash in between your birth and death to say? The best part, you get to choose what it says!

One of my favorite quotes by Dr. Maya Angelou is, *"I've learned that people will forget what you said, people will forget what you did, but people will never forget how you made them feel."* When people think of you, what feeling do you want them to have? I invite you to try this exercise: say your name (add your name) made me feel (add the feeling). Now, I want you to make this personal, and place how you want to make others feel. Yes, I want you to **ACT it Out!** Role playing helps you to see both sides of an argument because you are equally invested in both roles and not just your own feelings. Give this some thought. This is a great exercise to move toward gaining clarity.

Go deep! Where your passion lies your conversation will follow. When you love something you can talk about it continually with anyone, young and old. Your desires feel good and will light a fire inside of you. As you speak about it, a light shines on you and that light illuminates from the source that gave you breath. Trust that your desires came from a Higher Power. The talents that your Creator gave are dynamic and meant to produce not to collect dust.

I love the Parable of the Talents recorded in the Bible in the book of Matthew 25:14-30 ESV because it frames how many of us feel or treat our talents. Some of us feel we have one talent, 2, or 5 talents. The one who had one talent had a very different mindset than the other two that had more. The irony is they all had the same assignment and by the measure of their talent they were expected to produce.

This parable uses symbolic language to share the story of faith, progress, and the benefits of multiplying our talents. I encourage you to read it and see how God is the Master in this story. He had a serious conversation, a learning opportunity, for the three men who received talents. He expected them to multiply what He gave them. The two servants activated their faith, and one did not. What were the differences with these men and their outcomes?

The servants who multiplied their talents were blessed and received more from God. The servant who did not trust God or himself, buried his talent because he decided to play it safe. He held on to his talent but did not receive his blessing from it. God created humanity and then gave us the job to be fruitful

CHAPTER 1 | Trust Your Inner Desire.

and to multiply.

Our talents, when used properly, help us to evolve into something greater.

Like babies, they are born small, dependent, and ill-equipped for life but they grow and evolve into independent thriving adults. Trees start in seed form and just like a tree, our talents begin in seed form and when watered by our faith, they multiply. As you begin to reflect on your life, the stages, seasons, messages and nudges you've received, I want you to embrace this message and recognize the clues that are leading you to your purpose. This is where your strengths lie.

Acting was a strength and I had to start treating it like it. My gift made me unique and gave me my own way to relate to people, my activities, and God. I realized I could share my love of acting with my children as I played dress up, toy soldier, and sports. I had to channel my inner Lebron James to play basketball as I was not into sports growing up. I didn't stop there, I also used my gift at church when teaching Bible study and acting in plays. I loved the applause but even more so, the reflection people told me they had after the play. I cannot say how many times I have been in engineering meetings and broke the silence by saying, "Wake up! We are going to have fun today. If you guys are not willing, I am and will do it for the both of us if I must!"

Everyone would laugh and the room instantly became lighter and more inviting. As humans we can use our gifts in all kinds of settings if we are willing to think outside of the box. I am a mastermind with helping people look at themselves from a different vantage point. Sometimes it takes someone you trust to show you your mirror. As a coach and public speaker, I help people pull out their talents and repurpose them in a different way. The same way I was resourceful with acting, I teach my clients how to do the same thing with their buried treasures. Let's dig them up!

Too often, we do not take the time to define or think about our strengths. We focus on our weaknesses, lack, deficiencies, and deficits. We think from an empty cup and instead of emp

tying ourselves out day-to-day to be filled with new and fresh information. The servant with the one talent had the opportunity and ability to produce something more using that one talent, but he chose fear instead.

He hid his talent and hiding is rooted in fear. It is a learned behavior, a coping mechanism for too many of us. The wicked servant focused on fear instead of abundance. Where in your life are you focusing on fear and hiding from the good things that are desiring to come your way? A better question, why or how has fear gotten such a strong hold over you? An easy follow up question, do you want to be set free from the grips of fear?

What helped me discover my need to be set free from fear was the realization that I was accustomed to receiving validation on milestones I took. I was seeking validation from others and I didn't want that anymore. I didn't want to live in fear but I had to shift my mindset from what I was lacking to what God could provide for me. The moment I discovered the difference between my physical and spiritual strength was with the death of my father-in-law.

I saw him stop trying to be here in the natural world and look forward to the spiritual. I made a decision not to hide anymore in the physical because I learned that my happiness comes from within my spiritual connection and is not solely based on the physical realm anymore. My mindset shifted from outward things being the main reason I was happy, to recogniz-

CHAPTER 1 | Trust Your Inner Desire.

ing God. He increases my ability to produce the inner power that guides and guards my thoughts and regulates my emotions. Although the little things used to crowd my thoughts, today I see life from a higher place. I inherited happiness and peace as a child of God.

As a child, I thought I had to be perfect and say "yes" to everything, but I never said yes to God. Peace and happiness are mine and can be yours also! Growing up I loved to say yes, but I had to identify why I would say yes. If you are also asking yourself a similar question, "why do I do this or that?," I can say you are on a worthy path. My spiritual life brings me so much peace and calmness and I want to share how you can co-create to build your confidence in every aspect of your life. The things that happen in the world do not affect me as much as before. When hard moments come, I find comfort in knowing that this too shall pass.

The God that lives within me is my anchor. As long as I stay plugged into my power source I will remain focused, encouraged, and empowered to multiply my talents. Realizing that you can co-create and build the life you want by tapping into the divine, is a life changing discovery. You really can have your dreams and obtain what you ask for, if only you bring your spiritual existence to the natural world.

As I share my story, it is my wish and prayer that you find your unique talents. Ask yourself, what are my strengths? Take a moment to list your strengths. Without overthinking, allow yourself to be free, and list what comes to mind with no judgment. Be sure to mark the ones that really speak to you. I would love to know which ones resonate the most?

If you would like to share your thoughts in my Facebook group, "Tips to Live in Alignment," please join and post. I know for some of us, this may be a tall order. We may honestly be a fish out of water when it comes to answering questions like these. When I started this process, my answers were vague or dismissive. What I had to do to get real honest answers was to sit in silence with nothing playing on tv, no children running around, or my husband asking me questions. It was just me and my thoughts, experiences, and memories. Now, what is that thing (or those things) that you have or would naturally enjoy?

_____

_____

_____

_____

_____

Something I want you to do during this process, think about how you are feeling. Hold on to this joyous, light, and fuzzy feeling. Allow it to linger within your heart, mind, body, spirit, and soul. Did you know that your soul is your mind, will, and emotions? This euphoric high feeling should be the essence you want to leave with others. Write down the feelings that are associated with those talents. _____

_____

_____

_____

_____

_____

When we're children practicing the art of imagination came easily didn't it? As an adult, we have to find our child-like wonder and explore what we want to see. I had to relearn what I had already learned, that was taken away. When you live only thinking of outward things, you are robbed of your inner imagination. You are robbed of your creativity. What did your imagination allow you to create?

When you run a simulation for the growth of your talents through your imagination, envision who you are becoming in the process. Do you think the person you have seen in your inner self, could help your outer self do better than you are currently? Do you feel you can be able to trust this process? Do you trust yourself? Use this exercise to identify your strengths, embrace how it makes you feel, and envision what it looks like when you run a simulation for how your talents will grow in your future. Use this experience as a reminder to listen to the truth (the voice of the Divine) speaking to you in your inner self. Instead of being lured into distraction by external fear-based voices, listen within.

As you live out your spiritual experience, begin to trust the divine power living in you. Bring those old patterns to a halt. Mistakes happen, however remember you are not the mistake. Seek to enjoy life. Choose to bless the world with your talents. Be unforgettable. Leave your undeniable imprint by making an impact.

What impact will you leave in the hearts of the people you serve? When someone calls your name, what will they say about you? Give this some thought. One of my core reminders to myself is that *my inner self gets me*! It is the place where clarity and trust reside. She is my spiritual guide and she co-creates to make my outer self better. I trust I am protected, she offers me her best, and knows what's best for me.

I offer you an opportunity to tap into, stay present with, and get to know your inner self. Hear what your own voice is saying, then trust your own voice. Learn to discern your voice from the voices of others. I want you to master co-creating with your inner voice (thoughts and plans) and connecting with your outer self (your actions). Use the information in this chapter to practice hearing your inner voice.

Exercise 1

Considering your talents, write down five ways that you can influence and impact the people in your circle. **Act it Out!** "I will use my talents to impact the world…"

Step 1 Milestone Actions

1. List your talents from childhood to adulthood.

2. List your experiences that support your talents.

3. Identify which talents light up your smile.

4. List 3 strengths that you are known for.

_____

_____

_____

_____

_____

_____

_____

_____

_____

_____

CHAPTER 1 | Trust Your Inner Desire.

What has your Inner Voice Shared with you?

CHAPTER 1 | Trust Your Inner Desire.

Chapter 2

Identify Your Story.

"My experiences in life, whether good or bad, points to the test in my testimony."

– Charlene Harry

After enduring the challenge of trusting my inner talent and inner voice, I was able to identify why I made the choices I did. I determined that doubt, indecisiveness, or fear of failure was the reason. Feelings of failure were the largest emerging reason I made choices for a long time. I feared failing to reach my milestones so much I would abandon projects before I could witness failing.

I began thinking about my unfinished projects and unexamined ideas. I would start and stop projects that were important to me but because I felt rejected, defeat set in. The rejection made me feel worse as I thought about my failed attempts, unsuccessful experiences, disappointments, and unmet expectations.

CHAPTER 2 | Identify Your Story.

When I completed the steps from chapter 1, I recall thinking like the servant with the one talent. I devalued my talent because I could no longer simulate my future. I hid my acting talent to keep away from the embarrassment of failure and assimilate with the environment. I put acting on hold. Have you put singing, writing, drawing, or the things you liked to do on hold? If this rings true for you, know that you are not alone. The purpose of the first chapter is to call you into a trusting relationship with YOUR desires. Now that your desires have revealed themselves it's time to take action towards your goals.

I went to acting school and it was great, but it was hard to see myself in that industry. Although I enjoyed the process, I realized quickly, this wasn't how I wanted to spend my life. What I needed to master was how I can bring my love for acting to engineering which is what I enjoy most. Have you discovered a talent you liked as a child was not where you wanted to spend all of your time or make your career?

In order to trust your desires you must remember what they are. Let's face it, it is not an easy task to accomplish your purpose when you do not know what you were spiritually called to do. I lean into Genesis 1:31 where the Bible records, "God saw all that He had made was "Very Good."

The moment I began to trust myself, I fell in love with the learning process and the developmental phases of how to multiply my gifts and talents. I am still learning to multiply my talents. Sure, there were clues left along the way. My experiences became stepping stones instead of stumbling blocks. I encourage you to use your life experiences as reference points to how you can multiply your own talents.

Take a moment to dig a little deeper and review the experiences that left clues about your talents. Write down the patterns that you recognize that keep surfacing. How does it make you feel? Do you feel good? If so, why? Do you feel bad? If so, why? Notice what you can do to increase that feeling of goodness when the next opportunity comes around, or what you can do differently when faced with that same experience.

If you find it difficult to talk about how you feel, to get it out, I recommend Acting it out! Consider this fictional example or case and point. In the military, we often conduct After Action Reviews (AAR). This review and evaluation process are key markers of clarity and understanding an action, reaction, and consequence of an action. Reflect on your experiences and conduct your own after action review. Allow me to show you how.

Situation: A Team of 10 on a Student Event Committee were tasked to organize a College Music Festival.

Objective: The objective of the College Music Festival was to provide an entertaining and engaging experience for the student body, showcasing local talent, and fostering a sense of community.

Key Participants: Student Event Committee (10 members), Local bands and performers (5 acts), Campus facilities and security staff.

Key Outcomes:

- Attendance: Approximately 500 students attended the festival.
- Positive Feedback: Received positive feedback from attendees regarding the variety of performances and the overall atmosphere.
- Community Building: Students expressed a greater sense of community and connection with their peers

through this event.

Areas of Success:

- Planning and Organization: The event was well-planned, with clear roles and responsibilities assigned to each committee member. Regular meetings ensured everyone was on the same page, and tasks were completed on time.
- Talent Selection: The committee successfully curated a diverse lineup of local bands and performers, catering to different musical tastes and creating an engaging experience for attendees.
- Promotion and Awareness: Effective marketing strategies were employed, including social media campaigns, flyers, and class announcements. These efforts resulted in a good turnout and positive word-of-mouth promotion.

Areas for Improvement:

1. Logistics: The festival experienced some delays during setup due to coordination issues between the committee and campus facilities staff. Better communication and coordination protocols should be established for future events.
2. Sound Quality: While most performances were well-received, there were a few instances where the sound quality was subpar. The committee should invest in better sound equipment or ensure thorough sound checks before each act.
3. Crowd Management: The festival became crowded at times, causing inconvenience for attendees trying to navigate between stages and food vendors. Implementing a clear flow and designated pathways could improve the overall experience.

Action Items for Future Events:

1. Improved Communication: Establish regular communication channels with campus facilities staff and ensure clear expectations are set regarding setup and logistical requirements.
2. Quality Sound Systems: Research and invest in better sound equipment to enhance the audio experience for performers and attendees.
3. Crowd Control Measures: Create a layout plan for future events, including designated pathways, signage, and crowd management strategies to improve the flow and overall experience.

Conclusion:

Overall, the College Music Festival was a successful event that achieved its objectives of providing entertainment, showcasing local talent, and fostering a sense of community among students. By conducting this after-action review, the organizing committee identified areas of success and areas for improvement, allowing them to implement actionable steps for future events and enhance the overall quality of their initiatives.

Did you notice something about the format? Make a short list of actions and reactions. Don't get caught up in writing paragraph answers that can make things complicated. Keep it simple. Next, look at how every goal had a desired outcome. For every situation, there are opportunities to identify what went well, what could have been improved, and what actions can be taken to improve future endeavors. Practice using the AAR method to evaluate your progress and gather feedback to find your trouble areas and ways to improve.

Let's act out another scenario, a civilian life story, My Story, shall we?

CHAPTER 2 | Identify Your Story.

There was a time when I was complacent and I didn't see it as a problem. I was blind and did not realize I wasn't applying myself or using my multiple talents. I settled for my job and I thought I liked it. The truth, what I liked most was taking a 10 minute trip home for lunch! What seemed like happiness was actually convenience. I was content making less money because my job wasn't too stressful. So I did what most of us do when life is simple, I settled.

Settling in an unhappy environment is like a flower trying to bloom in a dark cramped room. No matter how much the flower tries to grow and blossom, the lack of sunlight and space restricts its potential, hindering its natural beauty and vibrancy. Similarly, when a person settles in an unhappy environment, their potential for growth, joy, and fulfillment is limited by the negative surroundings. They may feel trapped, stifled, and unable to express their true selves, which leads to dissatisfaction and unhappiness. Out of those experiences, hindrances, and adversities, I wrote the book "Stop Settling! You were Designed for Greatness." Just as the flower needs the right conditions to thrive, individuals also require a supportive and positive environment to truly flourish and find happiness.

I was numb, and my defining moment was after the birth of my long awaited third Child. At that moment, I took note of several signs. I was not in an environment that supported my deepest desire to truly make an impact that made life better for Soldiers. I wanted to leave a legacy for my children that created a sense of work life balance all at the same time. Although I had these desires, I was consistently denied the opportunity to grow in my career. I was encouraged to be someone that hid her talents in the workplace.

When I spoke to my graduating leadership development class, that was the moment I realized I wanted more. The positive feedback from my speech gave me clues that I could use my voice to impact others and help change their work life culture. I just was in the wrong position to carry out those intentions. So, I began applying for jobs and this action was a big step in the right direction. This step cultivated my focus and built my resilience to not let my love, dream, slip away and lay dormant. I became stronger as my response to being rejected for an interview or job offer. I did not stop after one or two attempts and not after hundred attempts. As you strive for your goals, it is critical to keep your eyes on the prize because life will test you. Be prepared for the tests and meet them with focus, determination, and resilience.

Realistic Expectations

If you were expecting to grab a book, buy a program, or latch on to someone else's story to build yours with no work, that is not having a realistic expectation. You must be patient with yourself and allow yourself to move forward no matter the speed. At times you may move slow and other times faster, but keep moving.

As you continue to gain personal clarity, try to equip yourself with bold expectations on your journey. When you looked at your AAR results I am sure you experienced a wide range of emotions to the hidden issues or obvious problems that were convenient to overlook. I know I felt disappointment, regret, out of place, left behind, and the need to run ahead to catch up, did you? Expect to experience raw emotions like fear, doubt, disappointment, sadness, and failure. The cycle of life will offer these experiences as agents to sharpen your tools, bring you focus, and most certainly give you clarity.

It's okay to be cloudy about the details and be on this journey of discovering answers. Remember that your previous experiences gave you knowledge and wisdom to respond to your new experiences. Continue to fearlessly fail forward. When your expectations are bold you will be equipped to handle anything that comes your way. You will not fall apart at the sign of trouble. You will not abandon your dreams because of adversity. *Let me tell you a secret, if you delete the "T" in can't you will experience life from a place of CAN!* Affirm it, now add an "I" in front of "can", repeat this to yourself, "I CAN". It's okay, get loud about this, feel it in your bones, believe it in your heart, "I CAN."

Exercise 2

Write out your limiting beliefs about your talents then read it aloud. Erase those thoughts and now write the truth. Next, write about your experience that illustrates your true ability and talents.

Step 2 Milestones Actions

1. Revisit your list of recurring experiences, what is being revealed about your talents?

2. Now, I want you to write what actually happened in a scene. You are going to write your own AAR featuring actors and Act it Out!

3. Take a look at what happened, then look at what you could have done differently? What will you do next time?

4. List a defining moment in your life when you wish you would have defended your talents instead of hid them.

5. Write your new response to doubt, fear, rejection, and disappointment.

Co-Create with Confidence

CHAPTER 2 | Identify Your Story.

What Past Personal Stories are coming to mind?

CHAPTER 2 | Identify Your Story.

Chapter 3

Self-Talk Is The New Self-Care.

"Self, I owe you an apology for every time I let self-doubt linger in my thoughts."

– Charlene Harry

Self-Talk is the New Self Care. Now, this is one of my favorite topics because oftentimes, people will catch me talking to myself. Thank goodness no one has tried to admit me to a mental facility. Is it just me that talks to themselves in third person–oh excuse me, "talks out loud?" "Yes, I talk to myself because it helps me think!" Or it is the actor in me that loves a good monologue. Don't judge me I promise I am not crazy, well maybe a little, aren't we all? Often, I have conversations with myself to the point it is second nature.

The truth I have learned, we all can benefit from talking out loud. Have you ever misplaced something and said, "Now, what did I do with my keys? I know I put them over here." Only you were not specifically talking to anyone in the room, but perhaps just you. Or you were talking aloud, addressing yourself. We all have that part of us that talks out loud, you see? So if I am crazy, we are now crazy together. LOL.

At first, it may seem strange to hear your own voice, but it's a normal part of cultivating a personal relationship with yourself. I enjoy talking to myself for more than one reason. When I get caught talking to myself, I say, *"If I can't talk to myself, I really can't talk to anyone else."* I have learned that when I can talk to myself nicely, I can talk to other people nicely. Sometimes you have to encourage yourself and speaking in your head is not enough, you need to hear a voice and your voice should be just as good as someone else's.

I love the story that was told by Dr. Wayne Dyer. Oh, how I wish I could have met him while he was alive. He shares a great analogy about an orange. Dr. Wayne Dyer was preparing to speak at an "I Can Do It" conference and decided to bring an orange on stage. He opened the conversation with a bright young fellow around age twelve who sat in the front row. He said:

"If I were to squeeze this orange as hard as I could, what would come out?"

The Young fellow looked at him like he was a little crazy and said, "Juice, of course."

"Do you think apple juice could come out of it?"

"No!" he laughed.

"What about grapefruit juice?"

"No!"

"What would come out of it?"

"Orange juice, of course."

"Why? Why when you squeeze an orange does orange juice come out?"

He may have been getting a little exasperated with Dr. Wayne Dyer at this point.

"Well, it's an orange and that's what's inside."

Dr. Wayne Dyer nodded and said, "Let's assume that this orange isn't an orange, but it's you. And someone squeezes you, puts pressure on you, and says something you do not like or offends you. And out of you comes anger, hatred, bitterness, fear. Why? The answer, as our young friend has told us, is because that's what's inside of you."

This is one of life's greatest lessons. *What comes out when life squeezes you?* When someone hurts or offends you? If anger, pain, and fear comes out of you, it's because that's what's inside. It doesn't matter who does the squeezing—your mother, your brother, your children, your boss, the government, what's inside of you will be what comes out.

What's inside is up to you, it's your choice.

The significance of this story is to call to your attention your words and reactions. This is an important life lesson to consider as you begin to analyze your responses to your life experiences. When your pressure points are poked, if you release anything other than love, check what you've allowed to get inside of you. What are your thoughts when reflecting on unsuccessful attempts of a desired outcome? What behavior patterns do you recognize? After you identify the negative thinking patterns that do not serve you, try replacing them with thoughts of love. Start loving on yourself in your thoughts.

When you set aside time to intentionally have a conversation with yourself you are, in essence, taking care of you. It doesn't have to be words you speak, but actions. Self-care can take on many forms: pampering, getting dolled up, taking a nap, or a little "me" time. Other examples include but are not limited to: quiet time, silence, reflection, hearing and tuning into your inner thoughts and listening to your inner voice.

My Story

As a Mom of 4, I often find it strange that I could be having a conversation in another room with my husband and mention one of childrens name who is intensively involved in watching a program in what feel is a far distance from the conversation at hand, but the minute their name is heard in conversation, their ears have tuned into that one thought mentioned in a separate conversation. My response is "This is an A & B conversation, please C your way out." In the same way I hear my inner thoughts having a conversation. It's as if there are millions of thoughts being spoken and I tune into the one that interests me. When I talk to myself, I become more aware of my beliefs. These beliefs influence and impact my thoughts on society's social and cultural constructs. Whether conscious or unconscious, I have become accustomed to my beliefs creating patterns that I live out through my habits. Have you noticed how your beliefs shape the patterns of your life? Do you value being organized and structured, so you bring that belief to how you live, clean, work, and etc?

There are words that I used to say over and over again. *"I ain't got time for that,"* was one of my favorite sayings. I didn't realize that by using this common phrase, I was conditioning my patterns, thoughts, and beliefs. The truth is, I have time for what matters most to me! Time is my resource. I no longer waste my time on empty words unless I digress, slip up and say it, but it is no longer a habit or a mindset that I practice. Deep and consistent conversations with myself help me to identify what is worth my time.

How often do you speak idle words that are not fueling you to think, be, or act positively? In this world where there are constant thoughts, words, actions, and opinions that can change your mind, it is important to have a consistent message. **Your voice matters!** There were and will always be other voices than my own that will seek to help, disrupt, interfere, and impede my growth. I have learned to take care of myself through the practice of self-talk; I learned to trust and honor my own voice. I know that people are well meaning and some people will try to write your narrative if you do not write your own. They say this is what you need to do; *go to school, get a job, get married, and have children, but what does your voice say*?

Self-talk will help you to bond with and trust yourself. The prompting may not be all the way ironed out, but listen to yourself and talk it through. You deserve to explore your own feelings about you. Begin asking yourself the right questions. Then listen for your answers because your answers are within you. I remember hearing my voice say, "I want you to apply for another job. I want you to have another child. I want you to write a book." I began to reason and wrestle with my thoughts and inner conversations. I was thinking in my head to apply for more jobs, but I didn't do it until I heard myself say it to me! I asked myself, "Is it ok to have another child?" and quickly said "yes" to me! What do you need to say "yes" to you about? Are you often saying "no" or doubting your voice? My inner guide led me to connect with my spirit during my talks.

CHAPTER 3 | Self-Talk is the New-Self Care.

> *"You have within you Everything you need to Create a Life without limits" - Charlene Harry*

Humanity has a pattern of seeking answers outside instead of inside. Before we listen to our own bodies, we entrust our physical care into the hands and expertise of a physician. When we are not feeling well, our bodies talk to us. Here is the principle, whatever the mind can't contain it imposes on our body. Here is the pattern: We get sick. We jump up and head to the doctor. When we get there, we are the experts being asked the questions.

If we feed the doctor our symptoms, he or she can in turn, with limited knowledge, prescribe medication or solutions. When we answer these questions we make it easy for the doctor to assess our condition. Have you made it easy for you to be the physician over your body? Have you been honest with your questions or answers to yourself? Or have you been neglecting yourself and falsely diagnosing yourself?

It is a best practice to pay attention to your body. Get into the habit of triaging yourself. Self-talk will help you to understand your body, its needs, and deficits more than anyone. In context, routine doctor visits are wise but no one trumps your knowledge of your OWN body. Too many have proven smarter than doctors when knowing themselves and diagnosing their problems. It is also true, some have believed answers about a condition that didn't exist.

Self-talk, the practice, helped me to identify self-doubt and non-affirming words like: "I can't do that, I'm not capable of this, I'm not like her, or there's no way that I could do that." I had to learn to use myself talk to challenge myself, yes, but also to affirm not discourage me. When I think crazy or speak aloud, my self-talk chimes in full swing, saying: "Excuse me... Did you try? Ok, how many times did you try? Do you know how many times they tried? What makes you think you cannot?" These conversations challenged the beliefs or thoughts that did not add value to my life. Today, when I have a limiting belief, I counter it by affirming self-talk.

I want you to know how I get clarity for myself when I hear opinions, beliefs, or thoughts of other people; I conduct a self inventory. I want you to have a conversation with yourself and Ask: Am I using my time wisely? Am I letting matters that are out of my control stress me out?

A few other questions you should also ask are: Am I true to myself? Am I achieving the goals that I've set for myself? Are you taking inventory? Do you question what you hear or run with everything you hear? How has that hurt you? Do you want to make it better?

If you want change–or better, you must change it. Start by paying attention to the thoughts that suggest you are not enough, inadequate, smart enough, educated, or that you messed up too many times, and do not have enough money. The list can continue on and on about the perceived lack. Hear them, but listen to your voice. What's coming up for you at this moment?

Self-talk is a spiritual conversation with God also. The physical experience is transferred into spiritual guidance. Ask yourself, what is my spirit guiding me to do, to stop doing, to say, or to refrain from saying. How can I co-create with my spirit? The power of talking to myself has been the conduit to becoming an entrepreneur, wife, and mother of four.

I spoke what I wanted in my life to myself first.

This process is not without challenges. I questioned and reasoned with myself first before deciding. I heard myself say, "Yes, that's what you should do. That's what you are meant to

CHAPTER 3 | Self-Talk is the New-Self Care.

do." It started with acting class, then getting married, and last launching my business. For you, it may be different. You may need to say yes I can pass this test, the next class, graduate, and get a great job I will love.

Ask and it is Given by Abraham Hicks is one of the main books that helped to tune into my spirit guides. It woke me up and helped me to realize that I have been speaking my desires into reality all my life. I began to recognize the power of saying, *"I am going to . . ."* I am an engineer. I am a real estate investor. I am a thought leader and book author. Those conversations propelled me to seek out what I desired in life. What should you be speaking into existence?

"I am" are two of the most powerful words in the universe. "I am" is one of God's names in the Bible. When I say it to me, about me, I am invoking that same power within myself. That divine power is being released by mere thought! You can do the same thing when you leverage your voice and start implementing your action steps with clarity.

I challenge you to take five minutes to write your "I am" statements. Write out what you believe about you, what you see yourself becoming, and what is true for you. Steer clear of what people want for you. Consider What are your core values and beliefs? What issues or causes in the world are you deeply passionate about?

Exercise 3

Begin to write out your "I AM" statements. Write your own story.

Step 3 Milestones Actions

1. Pick your top 3 I am Statements. I am_____.

2. Read Your Statements out loud in front of a mirror.

3. Believe what you are saying, and say it again with boldness.

4. Practice the ones that don't yet feel natural when you say it.

5. Don't be afraid to add to the List.

_____
_____
_____
_____
_____
_____
_____
_____
_____
_____
_____
_____
_____

CHAPTER 3 | Self-Talk is the New-Self Care.

Self Said What?

CHAPTER 3 | Self-Talk is the New-Self Care.

Chapter 4

Design Your Emotional Rollercoaster.

"Resilience is mastered through the ups and downs of life"

– Charlene Harry

Have you ever gone to the fair, stood in a long line, and anticipated the ride as you walked the guided tour of patience? You get to the front, finally, and you quickly shuffle into the front row and buckle in your seat. Then you have a pretty good thought that death is not likely, but it could happen. You take a chance, and you feel the breeze in your hair, the wobbliness in your bones, and your mouth can't seem to hide your instant terror as you drop, swing, and turn. You follow a track at lightning speed that someone else created for you and trust the process. Do you have the same grace for yourself?

Are you open to riding and experiencing the rollercoaster

CHAPTER 4 | Design Your Emotional Rollercoaster.

you can design for yourself? This topic is very important to me because I am very intune with my emotions. As a happily married mother of four children, from time to time, I tend to take a dive into my deepest emotions. When the emotions come, sometimes mental clutter, heartbreak, and sadness follows. When my thinking is clouded it disrupts my creative flow. I'm on pause for a moment, held in the balance of motion awaiting the next loop or turn. One of the biggest lessons I have learned is: Do not make important decisions when emotionally turning upside down on a rollercoaster! Refrain from making irreversible choices that will carry a heavy impact now and for years to come.

In the past, I experienced an inconceivable loss, the loss of my unborn child. This was one of the deepest dives my coaster has ever taken and the gripping feeling I felt as the wind left my mouth, and a sigh escaped. My husband was there to comfort me, but I still went through the motions of grieving a baby I would not be able to breastfeed, see run, laugh, or play. My husband and I experienced a hard hit together. We both took this dive together and I am glad I was not alone.

Have you had a terrible loss that sent you in loops, distracted your focus, or diminished your self confidence? Life is still happening around us as we are moving to energize talents and activate our plan. Losing people when you are away at school or working can be difficult and it is normal to grieve and even take some time off to be able to think and reflect.

In the midst of my miscarriage, I did not pause because I thought I was good; truly I tried to forget and numb my pain by taking a new direction to distract my heart. I made a decision that I should not have made at that time. I was able to recoup some of the money that I put down on a property, but I experienced a double loss.

What I thought would hide me from my pain, only led me to making more decisions at the time that revealed them. I came to realize, it was okay not to be okay. That lesson was a hard and fast one. I made a mental note: to never make a decision while I am emotionally charged or dropping. Likewise, when elevating, to still consider the cost because when my feelings subside, my choice would remain constant.

I reached for real estate when I needed to mourn, recover, and heal. I needed to pause but instead I used real estate as an escape and a mechanism to cope with my loss. Have you picked up a habit that was disguised to help you mourn, but only showed you more of your grief? Have you buried your head in the books only to fail an exam and not understand why? Or maybe you started a new relationship with someone who paid you no mind and made you feel alone or abandoned.

You can also take a job only to be reduced to a title. That title quickly loses its shine when your ambition and skill set is overlooked. There is a glass ceiling you now see that you didn't before. For others, it can be food. Some people try to eat to grieve loneliness or emptiness, but now you see your lack of self control in the mirror as you gain weight.

The grief was so much to bear. In my heart, I had a deep desire to have more children and that plan was shattered. A child was now missing from the family that we desired to build. An emptiness grew inside of me, my husband, my home, and my womb. My emotions and my body reminded me of the dream that was taken away from me. It was out of our control.

Have you wanted something so badly and it has not come to fruition? I know sometimes it is the college courses you wanted to attend, the apartment your heart was set on getting. Your problems may be different from mine, but the emotions we feel sends us on a roller coaster. In this case, the turns are

CHAPTER 4 | Design Your Emotional Rollercoaster.

not designed by you, and if they were, you are strapped in either way for the ride. We cannot control the ride but the response is up to us.

I did not like being out of control and not being able to do anything about it. I had to learn this valuable lesson to stay strapped into the process and respond appropriately to grief. For me, taking on a real estate project was something I desperately wanted to do to get back in control. In my grieving mind, I thought, If I did the real estate transaction it would make up for the loss of our child. In reality, nothing could replace the loss of our child.

At the time, I did not allow myself to acknowledge this truth. Instead, I latched onto the next desired goal without fully understanding that mourning was my next best action. Grief is a part of everyday life. Yet, oftentimes we are quick to deny grief in an honest attempt to live up to the "I am ok" coping response.

To release emotional turmoil, consider a few best practices I learned to help with the loss of my baby and feelings of defeat. I tried journaling, speaking my notes into my phone, and listening to them. I began talking to a therapist and a trusted friend, videotaping myself, and watching my recording also. These actions helped me see myself as I really was. I was so overwhelmed by my emotions, I stopped seeing myself and those whom I loved. I needed help to release, cleanse, rest, relax, and get clear. After a massive event in your life there may be a lot of emotional clutter all at once. How do you identify the emotions you're feeling at the moment? To get clear, sit with it, allow it to pass through, release it, and then when you're ready take inventory.

Sit with your inner-self to discuss your feelings. This is where the magic begins my friend. After you identify your feelings, take the time to ask, "Why do I feel this way?" Document your emotional responses to the question.

In the book *Ask and It Is Given,* Esther Hicks talks about different levels of emotions and how you can be at your lowest of lows and what you can do to get to the top of your desired emotion. It is a process. Know that you cannot jump to the desired emotion by merely saying it. If it feels false don't pretend, it only slows the process down. Stay true to your feelings. When you are not good, acknowledge it. Avoid going against your truth and do not say you are good when you are not.

My youngest daughter went on a roller coaster ride once. If only I could describe how big her eyes looked when she got off that ride. At the end of the ride and on the photoscreen she looked terrified. When the ride stopped, she was so scared and flustered she could not get out of the car. We asked her if she was alright, and over and over, she said, "I'm okay, I'm okay." But in reality, she was not okay. *It's okay to not be okay.* During times like this it is critical to recognize *Why* we are not okay.

It may be tough to acknowledge, understand, address or accept the truth but the truth is the only way to heal and move on.

Here are a few conversation starters to acknowledge your feelings. During this exercise: ask for what you need. Give yourself what you need at the moment.

- I just need a minute

- I cannot have this conversation right now

- Can we table this and come back to it

- I need to clear my mind
- I need to figure this out
- I need to be silent
- I need to breathe

This process will give you the space and time necessary to regain balance and emotional stability. Walking away from moments that overwhelm you is an act of self-care. I am a firm believer that your silence is more powerful than arguing or defending your point of view. Silence is your power. Use these practices to help you understand, embrace, manage, and regulate your emotions.

Abraham-Hicks' Emotional Guidance scale is used to determine one's emotional state, from highest to lowest.

1. Joy/Appreciation/Love

2. Passion

3. Enthusiasm/Eagerness/Happiness

4. Positive Expectation/ Belief

5. Optimism

6. Hopefulness

7. Contentment

8. Boredom

9. Pessimism

10. Frustration/Irritation

11. Overwhelming feelings

12. Disappointment

13. Doubt

14. Worry

15. Blame

16. Discouragement

17. Anger

18. Revenge

19. Hatred/Rage

20. Jealousy

21. Insecurity/Guilt/Unworthiness

22. Fear/Grief/Despair

Anger is an emotion that does not carry good or bad implications. Although anger is associated with a negative connotation, to be angry is to be human. With anger, the key is not to remain angry. Avoid rumination, revenge, and sulking; these are low vibrations and thoughts that lead nowhere good.

Get out of anger as quickly as possible because living in anger will block the process of emotional clarity. Do not focus on the past, because doing so will surely result in a crash. Use the past as a reference point to inform your present. Think about alternative perspectives and solutions. Invite God into your life throughout this process because God will affirm you and give you strength, clarity, and wisdom to respond to any situation.

Use this exercise to help you to regulate and manage your emotions:

1. Get Silent

2. Breathe

3. Identify your current emotion and be okay with not being ok in the moment

4. Visualize your desired emotion.

Recognize if you are angry and explore the root cause. Recognize if you are upset and try to see why. Discover what has you worried if you are worrying. Rephrase your thoughts if they are not leading to helpful solutions. This is the time when you acknowledge, *"Okay, I'm angry. This is why I'm angry. I would like to know my next best step."* The next step up might be realizing, *"I'm just a little disappointed," "I'm feeling a little overwhelmed, I can get through that,* or *I can get through this."* Just take it one step at a time to move up the ladder to a positive emotion.

A helpful factor to getting clarity about the emotional journey you need to take is to realize what emotion you want to feel. We have to be willing to let go of one emotion to embrace another. Get clear about the emotions that you desire. My desire is to always be at peace. It's one of my core values. Peace is given to us by God and it is also a choice. I experience peace when I am in alignment with my Divine Source. When I spend time with God there is peace in my heart, emotions, and decisions. Be firm in your approach to create space for your desired emotional state. Start to visualize yourself in that desired state because what you visualize you can realize.

I know a man who has a superpower and his name is my beloved husband. He is quiet and calm in nature. I haven't seen him get irate and lose control in the midst of tension even once. When tensions rise up, he is steadfast. It reminds me of Christ's level of calm when sleeping on the boat while the disciples were concerned about a ferocious storm. Matthew 8:23-27 explains that God calmed the sea using the power of his words.

When you fight against your emotions you will not win. Emotions will take you over if you deny its existence. Do the opposite, set the tone, set the atmosphere for peace to reign in chaos, confusion, and disagreements. Calm the storms that come your way with words that shape your environment.

Have you ever witnessed two people talking and one person is yelling and the other person responds without yelling? One reacts and the other responds. Sometimes, the calm person controls the power in the room and the person who is yelling will calm down. The calm person changes the emotional energy. You too can direct the emotional energy to create a win-win outcome.

"You did not come to face reality. You came to create reality." - Abraham Hicks

CHAPTER 4 | Design Your Emotional Rollercoaster.

Know that while you are going up and down this emotional rollercoaster you can assume creative license to design the ride. Recognize when you are about to go down on the emotional scale of fear or unworthiness utilize the tools shared to rise back up to love and passion. In each turn learn from the emotions you feel, and the responses taken to enjoy the ride. Remember, when you are dealing with a rollercoaster of emotions, you can remain empowered if you first bring yourself to a place of silence.

Emotional awareness is a core spiritual practice to bring you back to a position of clarity. When you are clear you can set your intentions and create strategies to navigate through life. Our emotions play a significant role in constructing our reality. Whatever streams through your mind eventually reflects in our personality and actions. Again, my desired emotion is peace, when I am angry, I instinctively know I am not in alignment with my divine source. When anger has power over my thoughts, my thoughts are not clear which can lead to the wrong action(s). With this knowledge, I must be careful about my thinking.

Thoughts help us to get clear and to co-create with confidence. There is a higher power, an inner guide within us, that desires to help us channel the power of our thoughts to attract what is best for us. Be aware of the messages that are coming through your emotional portals. Allow yourself to break through one emotion to your desired emotion. *Practice silence, meditation, and visualization.*

Exercise 4

Identify the most frequent emotions you experience. Write how you can move out of the scale of low emotions.

Step 4 Milestones Actions

1. Familiarize yourself with YOUR emotional scale.

2. Take a moment of silence to identify your current emotions.

3. Write down what is causing the emotions.

4. Identify the desired emotion.

5. Through visualization see yourself in alignment with your desired emotion.

_____

_____

_____

_____

_____

_____

_____

_____

_____

_____

_____

_____

_____

_____

CHAPTER 4 | Design Your Emotional Rollercoaster.

What Emotions are you facing?

CHAPTER 5 | Conscious Clarity And Its Connection To Time.

STEP TWO: ACTION

Chapter 5

Conscious Clarity and Its Connection To Time.

"My most memorable moments last a lifetime."

– Charlene Harry

Have you taken a time inventory lately? Or are you like the many who haven't thought at all about time? Most of us don't look at time until it is time to clock out, turn in a deadline, or complete something we wanted to end hours, days, months, or years ago. Did you know when we spend time identifying and connecting the dots between our conscious and subconscious desires, we gain clarity?

A recent study shows that 49 percent of people have never carried out a time audit which is considered a planning fallacy. The planning fallacy is one's tendency to underestimate the time required to complete a task or project. In essence, most people are not consciously aware of where they spend their

CHAPTER 5 | Conscious Clarity And Its Connection To Time.

mental, emotional, and physical time. People are busy doing things and not paying much attention to monitoring and tracking their personal and financial patterns.

Tell me would you have to think real hard, close an eye, and force your brain to envision a mental picture to recall how you spend your time or money? Assuming you have been tracking your spending and time, if I were to see the details, I could tell you what's important to you. Check out the article here by Acuity that shares how people are managing their time: Acuity Time Management.

Where are you spending your time? We all have 24 hours in a day. Is it a good representation of what or who you thought yourself to be? When you are spending your time, are you doing so where you want to? Or does your time management paint a different picture? Do you like what you see or has it brought clarity? When you take the time to identify how you spend your time you may not like what you see. Even if that is the case you should begin to see and analyze if your time matches your conscious and subconscious desires.

Do you find it odd that most people start and never finish their most important objectives? Why is this? It is called the "Attention Economy," coined by psychologist, economist, and Nobel Laureate Herbert A. Simon, who says it is the bottleneck of human thought. He goes on to say that *"a wealth of information creates a poverty of attention, and that limits both what we can perceive in stimulating environments and what we can do."*

In the manufacturing world, a bottleneck is a hard stop that slows down the timeline efficiency of a project. The bottleneck is the first area that needs to be addressed to get back on track. I love the clarification that is made in the definition of the attention economy which states it is the "bottleneck of human thought." To gain clarity on your next best move, you first need to revisit the thoughts that are blocking your ability to carry out your desires. Take a moment to consider the external factors that overstimulate your thoughts, limits your perception, and impacts the flow of your projects.

Social media is one of the most prominent sources of overstimulation. People are addicted to their cellphones and being constantly pumped full of information. 24 hours out of the day, rain or shine, home, college or at work. Some people even bring their phones into the bathroom to stay constantly connected to their phone for information. Social media surely exposed an over saturation of content and the desire for people to stay informed, but now to a fault. We used to say but not completely believe television destroys brain cells, but society has clearly taken a different approach since media has become mainstream.

Ten seconds on social media can turn into ten hours with a constant finger swiping up or letting each video autoplay. I remember when COVID started and the term Netflix binge-watching became a thing. Many of us sat down to watch tv and pass the time, only to watch one episode after another until before we knew it we finished the series in one or two sittings.

An equally dangerous and common stimulation is going into the grocery store to get one or two things and coming out with fourteen or more instead. Our minds become overstimulated with information, images, ads, graphics, and pictures. This flood of information grabs our attention and then pushes our intention outside of our visual radar. Another example is how you can see a big menu and be more perplexed on what to order than if you had fewer items.

In the words of Theoretical Physicist Michael Goldhaber, *"Information is not scarce, attention is."* Our attention span is short because we are overloaded with stimulating information. This is why it is important to connect with your inner guide

CHAPTER 5 | Conscious Clarity And Its Connection To Time.

daily. The only way to get clarity is to spend time thinking about your goals. As I mentioned in my free mini-book, *5 Tips for Living Your Best Life*, I point out how taking the time to focus on your desires will best serve you when you practice them daily.

Now, I want you to consider how new information affects your end goal? Does the new details add value? Or, are you spending more time sifting information instead of taking practical tips to see a desired outcome? Are you making the most of your time, or are you really busy being busy? Are you multiplying the information you receive to feel like you are moving forward when in fact the waters around you are the only thing moving you into a direction like sand at the beach? If you stand still in the sand in shallow waters, you can still drift away from your goals.

In order to not be lost at sea, you must keep your eyes on your desired destination and not allow the sights to distract you. Should we enjoy our view, sure, nothing is more beautiful than seeing a coastline or the sun setting on the water with a view of an infinity natural pool of water. However, are you being dazed by pretty pictures that have you looking into the stars instead of reaching for them?

How often do you sit and watch tv or social media? An even better question, what insights do you gain from watching a show, listening to a video, or podcast? Everything we do impacts our clarity or the lack thereof. I do not like horror stories because I do not see how they will help me to get to where I want to go. Plus, they are good for making you hyper paranoid, scared of the dark, and seeing things that are not there. If we are distracted by things we can see, why waste attention on chasing horrifying fantasies?

I know some people who like horror because they spice up their what they call "boring life," but would you agree that there are better ways to get a jolt of energy and surprise? Let me know what you like to do to keep your life spicy, fun, and exciting. Post them in [my Facebook group](#) and be sure to join if you haven't yet. Now, I get it, life can get boring or monotonous if we work, cook, clean, and do the same old thing day in and out. So how do you enjoy spending your time?

If you say "watching tv," I won't be mad or judge you, but I would ask, is there something better you could watch that can keep your attention and lead to your dreams? I watch tv too, but I did a tv inventory and realized my tv watching for entertainment had to be shrank a great deal if I wanted to remain clear and focused on my desires. The bottom line is the things that add the most value are the areas I choose to spend the most time.

Be very conscious of what you hear and see because those things will impact how you move through time. They will either draw you closer or move you further away from your goals. So take a time inventory and be honest with what you find, but don't stop there, take some intentional steps to fix the problems you see.

Again, the truth is 82% of people do not have a time management system which is why most people don't know where they are spending their time, reports Acuity Article. A lack of time management not only heightens mental health issues due to high stress levels, poor sleep habits, and burnout, but it also costs business owners tons of money each year. How can a person be effective at their job if they haven't slept well in weeks? How can they take their job seriously if they are living a fantasy life in their heads that seems more attractive to their reality.

Most people like virtual worlds, avatars, online chats, text messages over phone conversations and human interaction. This virtual world is not limited to phones and computers but

CHAPTER 5 | Conscious Clarity And Its Connection To Time.

includes 3D goggles and maze games where people can explore living an alternative lifestyle with a real appeal. Social media and TV also allows people to live other people's lifestyles through the programs they watch, the influencers they follow, or the video games they play. As you begin to look at your life, it is important to take inventory of how much time you spend looking at the real you, your life goals, and ambitions.

Back to the importance of a time audit, it will help you schedule these necessary check-ins. Have you taken a moment yet to conduct a personal audit? If not, now is the time to get going in the right direction. During this step into clarity, you are going to complete a time audit. Start thinking about what you have been watching. First, reconsider what you spend your time on and how much time. **Consider the value that time is bringing back to you**. If you had to put a value on it, not everything is monetary yes, but does it bring you joy, clarity, or hope? Has it added to the quality of life for you? If so, explain.

_____

_____

_____

_____

_____

Next, I want you to spend some time looking at your goals. I know most of us look at our goals once a year in January. Goals can make most of us turn in our stomach because goals can point a finger to our true identity. We cannot hide from our own goals when we write them down and look at them often. Looking at them often, however, doesn't have to be a bad thing, it can be a motivating factor instead.

Break up your Goals into three categories:

1. What are your goals for your Mind, Body, and Soul?

2. Looking at your relationships with your Self, Partner, Family, and Friends, what goals do you want to set?

3. In your Career or Business, what goals have you avoided setting?

_____

_____

_____

_____

_____

_____

My mental state is the most important category that helps me with my goals and the legacy I desire to leave behind. It's what drives my actions to fulfill my goals in my relationships and my career. My family is very important to me, However, if I don't pour into myself, it makes it harder for me to pour into my family. I cannot give to someone else something that I don't have within myself.

Self-care is a real thing and you need to be clear that taking it is not robbing someone else. It is the maintenance that ensures your engine keeps going to help others in need. I take care of myself by including things that make me happy. What I watch and listen to aligns with my mental and physical goals.

Another aspect of self-care is self-worth. If I say I love

CHAPTER 5 | Conscious Clarity And Its Connection To Time.

you and don't give you any of my personal time, or undivided attention, how can you be sure? I value my relationship with my husband and he is very important to me. We maintain our relationship by intentionally investing our time into our marriage. We are sure to keep our date nights and not allow children, career, or business to stop us from connecting.

What about you? Do you make time for your parents, siblings, and friends? Or are you so busy studying and pursuing your dreams that you put everyone on the back burner? There is a time that you need to be focused, however, being focused doesn't mean abandoning people you love.

Four important relationships I care a lot about are the ones I have with my children. I have four wonderful children and I make it a priority to spend time with them collectively and individually. I like to hear their dreams, celebrate their victories, and know their challenges. This small but time consuming gesture is how I show them their worth to me. The time I give is just as important as the money I pay to care for them.

In addition to my relationship goals, I have career and business goals as well. I have to give my undivided attention to my career goals and milestones while at the job. If I do not, my personal life will block the value I desire to bring to work. Leaving home, I table unresolved issues until a better time to discuss it. I've learned to separate business from my home life. If I don't clear my head, I find those feelings and emotions can play-out at work and I could blow-up on the wrong person. My life is very busy, yes, and without proper time management, everything would stop and I would be totally miserable with nothing good to report.

The three categories listed above are examples of my priorities, but they may not be yours. This list can and should be customized to fit your priorities. The goal is to allot time in your day, in your week, and in your month to conduct this time audit regularly. This process will give you insight and help you to analyze if your choices match your words and desires.

The self-audit is designed to be an eye opener. Just like looking at your bank statement you can see your spending habits, this time audit will show you where you are spending your time. When you look at the numbers, treat it like you would your money. You would ideally determine where the value is, what should I do more of, less of, or cut out all together. Now that you know, it is time to take action.

I realized that I'd rather spend time on things that add value to my legacy. Do you think now is a good time for you to be building your legacy? I want you to take this challenge seriously because time management is what you need to build your legacy and confidently accomplish your goals. This is your chance to think about how you can make the most of your time. Skipping this process and even reading the rest of this book, will backfire. This list of goals will be a springboard to help motivate you to keep on this journey to clarity.

When my husband and I started in real estate, it was scary because we didn't know what we didn't know. We had to immerse ourselves in the process and invest in training programs, coaching programs, and YouTube University. Networking, Trial and Error was the key and the core of our growth and development. The good news is the work we put in has paid off. To get here, we had to put down entertainment, we had to watch Youtube videos on real estate when I wanted to watch something just for fun. I had to trade off my wants to get my desires! I encourage you to spend the time and set goals so you can obtain your desires.

Now one beat of caution I do have to tell you, goal setting is not picking a lot of random things and trying them all at once. Have you ever invested in something that you did not use

CHAPTER 5 | Conscious Clarity And Its Connection To Time.

immediately or at all? How did that make you feel? Did you feel like you wasted your money, time, or resources? It's important to me to make a good return on my investments (ROI). It is senseless to invest in something that you do not use or allow your hard-earned money to sit around and collect dust. Do not waste your inventory, energy, and space on something you know you are not going to follow through with accomplishing.

I also have to mention, what you buy has to live somewhere. Physical items need shelves, closet space, and thoughts even need mental shelves. Do not waste your resources on things that you could live without. My process is not perfect, but it is a great place to start and adapt to your needs. To be honest, I have unread books and unapplied information that I must decide what to do with. What things and ideas do you now have to place somewhere or give away? That's right, get rid of these distractions. As you consistently move in the direction of your desires it is equally important to set aside or completely remove things that do not support your goals.

Confidence is built upon the actions and experiences that we live through. Life is the best qualifier of your abilities, not your education, family status, or social placement. Real estate was intimidating because of the unforeseen challenges I had to face with contractors, property managers, and even tenants, but I overcame it and you can too! Being in college, employed, single, or married all come with challenges! I had to step into real estate to know that my experience was enough for me to have a confident voice for what I desired. When you look back at your resume and experiences, reflect on what you've done– not just well- but also mistakes taken.

Examine what you have overcome as a quick self-check for you. I need you to reflect on this right now, so that you can build your confidence. This practice will lead you to the clarity you seek and that clarity will lead you to confidence. Don't dwell on your struggles and challenges but instead remember your good works and your triumphs because they are the conduit to confidence. _____

_____

_____

_____

_____

_____

The National Sleep Foundation advises that healthy adults need between seven and nine hours of sleep per night. In the guidline they published they posed the question and answered the question, How much sleep do we really need? Consider how much time you spend sleeping, working, and on pleasure. Is your life balanced in a way that each category is divided evenly into eight-hour blocks (8 sleep, 8 work, 8 pleasure)? I look forward to hearing about the changes you will make within your three 8-hour blocks of time.

Lastly, I have to tell you it is important to give yourself grace. Earlier, I mentioned that this exercise made me feel pretty bad when I first did the time and life audit. When I learned that I did not spend my time wisely it was like a kick in the butt–no a slap in the face! I am still practicing this system and giving myself grace as I learn. Be graceful with yourself in this process as well. You are learning and growing and that is a cause for celebration and recognition. Clap for yourself!

Exercise 5

Define your Life Goal Categories. What actions support or distract you from your Career & Life Goals

Step 5 Milestones Actions

1. Review my goals list, but adapt the list to fit your goal categories.

2. Commit to doing this time audit within the next 24 hours, and follow up at least weekly until you develop the habit of being honest and consistent.

3. Quantify how much time you spent in your goal categories.

_____

_____

_____

_____

_____

_____

_____

_____

_____

_____

_____

_____

_____

_____

_____

_____

Where do you desire to Spend Your Time?

CHAPTER 5 | Conscious Clarity And Its Connection To Time.

Chapter 6

Confidence Connects With Actions.

"No One can take away my Truth."

– Charlene Harry

Building on the steps to Co-create with Confidence, let's do a quick review to see how well you are progressing through the book so far. The good news, you are ALMOST done! Can you believe it? I trust you will connect with me before you go!

Okay, back to the review, we discussed the importance of knowing your desires as they align with your talents according to the spirit. In chapter two, we identified experiences that support our desires. In chapter three, we learned the importance of practicing self-talk which lends itself to confidence when we are co-creating our desired goals. In chapter four, we talked about the emotional roller coaster that we will experience due to overstimulating environments that impact our experiences.

CHAPTER 6 | Confidence Connects With Actions.

These four steps are the foundation to getting your Clarity. Most recently, in chapter five we discussed clarity and its connection to time.

Have you been noticing that your confidence is building as you practice and complete each chapter? I want you to focus on the milestone actions because each one builds upon the previous milestones. When you understand your experiences, it forms motivation to take more action. Continue to develop your skills in this chapter of the book and pat yourself on the back.

I am sure if you are like how I used to be, as you go through the process of developing your skills, you may begin to compare yourself to others using their achievements as markers for your own. Do not compare yourself to anyone because we all have different starting points and needs. *Comparing your journey with someone else's is akin to self-abuse.* The underlying belief is that someone is better and more valuable than you. That's covert abuse. Trust that opportunities will meet you when you're ready. Know that preparation plus action will lead to triumphs.

I remember when I finally got a position in the government after moving to a new state to join my husband. I was bombarded with thoughts and sayings from the staff. I was told, "You are going to have to wait your turn. Don't be surprised if it takes you longer than 2 years to get promoted. It's nothing personal, it is just the system." I am sure they also thought when I walked into their "good ol' boy network," "Who does this girl think she is attempting to bust up our groove? Does she really think she is going to come in here and change how we do things?"

Even though the dogs were barking, I believed in my ability and expertise to effect positive change within the first quarter of the year. I started to increase my skills and knowledge in areas they had no knowledge about. Positioning myself as a valuable asset not only improved their processes but also worked to help the soldiers we served. People began to take notice of my value, talent, and ingenuity. They began to witness my capabilities and appreciate my talents. I was attracting more opportunities that increased my skills, and that got me seen all the more.

During this time, I applied for positions and even though I did not receive a call for an interview right away It did not stop my personal and professional development. I was leveraging my time by adding intellectual property to my resume and talents. I double downed on what I was doing and sought to learn and master more of my Six Sigma skills. I knew that if I continued to build up my time, project management, and problem-solving skills, I would be of higher value here or elsewhere soon enough.

If you find it takes time to get placement after you graduate, don't get discouraged. If you are on a job and finding it hard to advance, don't get discouraged. Keep working on you because your promotion will come soon enough if you keep leveraging to capitalize on your talents and voice.

After I completed my professional development, I decided to get serious about finding a suitable environment to use my skills. I was determined to make some changes in my level of responsibility and finances. After I submitted 167 job applications, I secured three job offers, two promotional and one lateral. This is a good demonstration that opportunity meets the one who is ready and persistent. I am so thankful that I seized the opportunity to prepare myself to leverage my time by developing myself professionally.

Never think that the time you spend working on you is a waste of time. Sometimes our dreams, goals, and desires take a minute to catch up with our planning; but when the two meet, fireworks and magic happens. I was ready for my elevation be-

CHAPTER 6 | Confidence Connects With Actions.

cause I did the work to build my confidence, and co-created my alignment by putting action behind my desires. Wishing doesn't change your life nor does negative self-talk, harsh judgment, and discouraging words.

I secured a new position and I received two promotions in less than two years. I moved from a toxic environment to an environment that complimented my value. Sometimes you have to leave the space you are in, and if you are in that environment, try to pull what you can before you leave. If I hadn't taken that time to work on Charlene, who is to say if my next chapter would have ever started as soon as it did.

I was able to step into the next chapter of Charlene Harry because I didn't quit in my previous chapter! I connected my confidence with my actions, and I received great results that I also believe many of you will have as you continue this process. Have you ever been so close to something you could taste it? This is the time too often people also give up, resist doing that. Remember, confidence plus actions will equal great results.

Yes, there will always be challenges no matter what phase of life you enter, but resilience results all the more when you fight with your actions, tenacity, and consistency. The truth of the matter is, I graduated from a predominately White Accredited University not only being among the handful of minorities attending, but as a woman also! I would have been a double "no" to some but I earned a Six Sigma Green Belt from the one and only, General Electric Company, when Jack Welch was in charge!

No one can take away your experience, work ethic, heart, skill, confidence, talent, or clarity when you put in the work. You have to decide to give it away! No one can take away the strength that you put into your experience. When you continue to focus on your strengths and increase your skills, I call that your ***Superpower***.

Comfort Zones

What is the nemesis to your superpower? Your comfort zone. Yup, your greatest threat to your progress is not someone else, but you! There is a universal conversation around the topic and ironically, everyone is on the same page. If you are living in your comfort zone, people will say to you, "snap out of it." Although people may tell you to move out of your comfort zone quickly, I say take your time, take in what you see, but stay active. Stretch yourself while you're there to reach your desires.

The same way you warm up before you start a workout, you should do while in a comfort zone. Rest assured, this state of comfort will not last forever. Evolution is inevitable. Whether you move up or down in life, life will still evolve. Your skills either increase, lie dormant, or decrease in an area. To build confidence, adopt the stretching mentality to expand your comfort level and comfort zones. We have to learn to get comfortable with challenging ourselves in healthy ways.

When you continue to learn and evolve on a particular task you will build strength. Your newly found comfort zone should be one that makes you okay with being where you are but stretching for where you want to go. I've always been comfortable speaking, but I'm stretching myself by speaking to more people at once and on topics that are personal to me. By putting myself on different platforms, visiting colleges, and speaking at business functions for companies I'm stretching myself. This is a vulnerable space for me and I am sure stretching for you too may feel uneasy. However, if I operate from a place of strength then vulnerability, I can find comfort in the stretching. Build on your strengths and manage your weaknesses.

Exercise 6

Discover what talent(s) you will build upon that align with your desired goals. Become the expert in your talent.

Step 6 Milestones Actions

1. What is something you had to work very hard to accomplish or receive?

2. Which goal areas will help stretch you while in your comfort zone?

3. If you are in college or on the job and you are thinking about the next step, challenge yourself to make the most of the here and now. Look for what you can do to make the most use of this comfort zone.

4. Write your answers down and determine a plan to execute the next move to achieve your goal.

_____
_____
_____
_____
_____
_____
_____
_____
_____

CHAPTER 6 | Confidence Connects With Actions.

What are fruit producing Actions?

Co-Create with Confidence

CHAPTER 7 | Co-Create With Infinite Intelligence.

STEP THREE: RESULTS

Chapter 7

Co-Create With Infinite Intelligence.

"Breathe Deep and Quiet the Mind."

– Charlene Harry

You did it. You are at the final chapter where we talk about how you can co-create. This chapter discusses how you can co-create with infinite intelligence, which Napoleon Hill describes in *Think and Grow Rich.* He wrote that, "Infinite Intelligence is the force that gives order and origin to everything in the entire universe. It is the prime source, the first cause of everything that comes into existence."

My ongoing prayer is that God will give me this level of clarity. It is also my prayer that you gain clarity on what steps you will take after this book. There may come a time when you doubt or are unclear about your next move. Similarly, you may not be sure if you are doing the right thing. Just know, as you move within and toward your milestone action, you will use everything you learned to gauge your progress in proximity to your desired goals.

If the action you take and the skills you develop will get you closer to your goal, then it's the right thing to do. Not every step will look right but it can be made to help you along. All things can work together for your good if you maintain that clarity on the matter.

Everything that helped you in this book, especially the after-action review tool that I shared in Chapter 2, use it. Ask yourself and be honest, "What's Working? What could you have done better? What action will you choose next time?" If you still question whether or not you are in alignment with infinite intelligence, allow me to help you identify if you're in alignment. It is called 'signs' also known as confirmations that you should search for. Confirming signs indicate that you're moving in the right direction of your desired goal.

Have you ever experienced something that came along by surprise that is in alignment with what you want to do? At different intervals in my life I have had this experience. I am thankful that I've been able to allow the action of infinite powers to assist me in aligning with what is meant for me. Universal Abundance is looking to co-create with us. I will say that again! *The Universe desires to co-create with you, you do not have to go at it alone!*

The words you speak into the universe can pull what you desire closer and closer to you. The thoughts you have in your mind or the feelings you feel in your heart can also push you forward. Your experiences can serve as reminders for what you survived, learned, and conquered. You are not defeated because it took you longer than someone else, the whole point is you made it!

Although the universe is seeking to co-create with you, the obstacles will still come. It rains on the just and the unjust all the same. Those that believe and those that don't get chances and glimpses of understanding the Higher Power. Learning to navigate in the world using wisdom is based on your divine connection to the source energy which is God. You may be subject to a toxic non-supportive low vibrating environment where people say things like "Woe is me, there's no way out, or it can't be done." In the past, I created and supported a toxic environment in my mentality that cost me during different times in my life.

I have learned when people are talking to me they are holding up a mirror to themselves. Unsolicited advice, opinions, critiques, and judgements come with knowing people. I learned to separate their concerns from the concerns that God has for me. I know the God I serve has plans to prosper me, and not to forsake me. The good life is easily accessible if we remain connected with Infinite Intelligence and allow the love from the Universe to reveal our path.

Now that you have discovered your talent to multiply, know that as you become a servant leader, the life you desire is within reach. There are a lot of moving pieces to reach your ultimate goal. As you move forward and navigate uncertain waters, understand that you may not have all the answers. It's ok. Yet if you trust that the Creator gave you your desires, trust that your actionable steps will build one after another. If we allow the Universe to fill in the gap on some of the how to's, the signs will appear. When we can see the light at the end of the tunnel, it will create the momentum to bring us closer to our goals. Keep the momentum, watch for the signs, and keep your eyes on the light of the Creator.

On a subconscious level, I am connected to the infinite abundance in the universe. My spiritual guides are tuning into my thoughts. The universe responds to my thoughts that manifest in the physical world. That's the simplicity of co-creating with the infinite source, it doesn't have any objections to what is in the unconscious discussions. So if you say I'm broke, you will remain broke. If you say, I will never be able to get a promotion. You will never get a promotion. The universe aims to give you what you believe you can have.

It is important to recognize the subconscious conversation in addition to the conscious conversation you are having. Oftentimes when there's a conflict between the conscious and the subconscious our progress slows down. It takes longer to see our desired goals realized when we are double minded, going forward and backward at the same time.

When you are in this weird holding pattern, it is important to listen to your internal conversations. Unspoken prayers are powerful. Even in silence, God hears our prayers and internal conversations. The Creator desires to have conversations with you. In the book of Philippians God emphasizes the importance of what we should think about. Philippians 4:8 tells us to *think about things that are true, noble, right, pure, lovely, admirable, excellent, and praiseworthy*. When we fix our thoughts on these things we can navigate through life with confidence and clarity. This is where his thoughts reside and if you tap into his abundance, frequency, and vibration, you will receive your earthly blessings.

Be conscious and clear about what you allow yourself to think. If you say, I can't, you can't, if you say I will, you will. That is instant co-creation. Strive to maintain a positive mindset. The challenge is to rethink any thoughts that do not add any value to your desired goals.

As you begin this exercise, think about how your thoughts align with the thoughts listed above. Use the exercise below to identify your thought life.

Exercise 7

Take notice of your internal conversation between your conscious and subconscious dialogue. Notice conflicts and agreements.

Step 7 Milestones Actions

1. Identify the signs in your daily milestone actions.

2. Recognize the conversation between your conscious and subconscious talk.

3. Rephrase any thoughts that do not add to your desired goals.

4. Identify any new milestone actions you can take to get closer to your goal.

5. Rewrite your talents and gifts down and consider how to leverage them to capitalize on your goals.

_____
_____
_____
_____
_____
_____
_____
_____

CHAPTER 7 | Co-Create With Infinite Intelligence.

CHAPTER 7 | Co-Create With Infinite Intelligence.

What Notes are in sync with your Inner Voice?

Chapter 8

(Bonus Chapter) Manifest Your Desires Daily.

"My energy flows where my desires go."

– Charlene Harry

This bonus chapter provides a summation of how you can manifest your desires on a daily basis. Come take a glance at my signature packet *Empowerment T.E.A.* These three impactful ingredients are needed to make your very own Personal Empowerment T.E.A. This is a guide to make life more favorable and comforting. I sip on these three ingredients daily to stay focused on my life goals and to align with my divinity.

The first ingredient that goes into this empowering routine is called *Trust*. The T stands for *Trust*. I cannot speak enough about trust because we have been forewarned to not put our trust in man. When I put my trust in the Creator of all things, I cannot be disappointed. Sure, I may not get exactly what I want, yet I trust that God knows what is best for me. He gives me my desires and the means to carry them out.

CHAPTER 8 | (Bonus Chapter) Manifest Your Desires Daily.

Your desires are uniquely your own. The first chapter discusses the power of your desire which was given to you by God. Remember, your desires are not just for you, but also for you to give as a servant leader utilizing your talents. What God has given you to do, He has equipped you to do. 1 Corinthians 10:13 says, *God will not give you more than you can handle*. Know that whatever he gave you, he knows you can handle it. He is working inside of you to help you perform it.

The second ingredient that goes into this empowering routine is called *Enough*. The E stands for *Enough*. This special ingredient says wherever you are in life is enough. Be content where you are right now. Be in the here and now. Where you are is where you need to be. Avail yourself to your teachings and lessons on this level. Learn to integrate and implement your learning here before you move to the next level.

Today's outcome is a result of yesterday's experiences. As you grow and learn, give yourself grace when you do not handle life the way you wanted or needed. Be gentle with yourself. Revisit chapters to enhance your knowledge as you continue to grow and evolve on this journey. Be settled with knowing that this moment is enough.

I love the statement that success leaves clues. Take a look into your past and look for clues to your success. Spend at least 15 minutes at a time to think about your defining moments. Consider how those moments helped you grow. Then, how can you continue to grow?

The third ingredient that goes into this empowering routine is called *Alignment*. The A is for *Alignment*. Align your milestone action to the goals that you want to accomplish. Examine your actions to see if your choices are moving you in the direction you are destined to go. How you manage your time plays a significant role in alignment. The "A" stands for alignment, actions, and allow. The alignment of your actions allows the universe to align with your desired outcome.

Sip on your Empowerment T.E.A. daily as you apply these three ingredients to your life. Trust that you are enough. Trust that you can align your actions to your desires and the Universe will help you realize your desired goals when you allow the signs and power within to make a way.

I implore you to complete the milestone actions at the end of each chapter. I want to remind you to conduct your very own time audit occasionally to compare your results to your previous. Get to work on becoming an expert in co-creating with clarity and confidence. Build on your skills and learn to leverage your unique skills to serve others. I am super excited that you have gotten this far. I know that you are serious about gaining and receiving the clarity that build your confidence. Trust the process as you find YOUR clarity and co-create with confidence to capitalize on your talents and achieve your desired goals.

Until we meet again, I wish you all the best that life has to offer.

Charlene

P.S. email or scan and give your review here for a free gift!:

or send a email to: contact@charleneharry.com and get the video introduction and mini-book Empowerment. T.E.A *free* (*$55 value*) when you provide a review of this book.

LET'S KEEP IN TOUCH

E-mail your "aha" moments and get a free digital copy of how to make your own Personal Daily Empowerment T.E.A.

contact@charleneharry.com

Book Me as a Speaker

I would love to speak at your next student / employee leadership program or corporate function. Please visit my website to learn more.

www.charleneharryspeaks.com

CHARLENE HARRY'S RESOURCES

To access any of the resources below go to:
www.successwithcharlene.com

Free Resources

Ready to leverage and capitalize on your talents ?

- *Claim your free pdf: 5 Tips for Living Your Best Life!*

Get weekly tips to Peace and Productivity hacks when

- *Join my email weekly Newsletter*

Join the community that Stays in Alignment with their Wisdom to Wealth

- *Join my Facebook group: Tips to Live Inspired*

Paid Resources

If you want to speed up your results to engage your talents, gifts, and quickly learn to leverage your skills to earn more do this. Invest the time to find your clarity, increase your voice, and make decisions with confidence when you take my 8-week expedited course.

- *Take the 8-week Course*

Book a 15 minute call to apply for admission into a private 1 on 1 virtual mentor session with Charlene Harry. She will help you quickly find the talents you thought would be of no use and teach you to leverage them for great results. Bring your work and life into balance with this breakthrough session and set the trajectory of your legacy. Serious inquiries only.

- *Go deeper with me as your Coach*

For more information on the above go to
www.successwithcharlene.com

Thank you again for reading!

To get your free intro video and book download of Making your own Personal Empowerment T.E.A.

- *Submit a review to this Email: contact@charlene-harry.com*

WORK CITED

Chapter 4

Hicks, Esther; Hicks, Jerry. *Ask and It Is Given: Learning to Manifest Your Desires.* Hay House; 1st edition (1 April 2004)

Chapter 5

Richardson, Ben. Time Management Statistics & Facts. Acuitytraining.co.uk, 26 October 2022, *acuitytraining.co.uk/news-tips/time-management-statistics-2022-research/Acuity Article*. 16 Feb 2023

Suni, Eric. "How Much Sleep Do We Really Need? "National Sleep Foundation. *www.sleepfoundation.org*, 7 March 2023, sleepfoundation.org/How Sleep Works/How Much Sleep Do We Really Need? 7 March 2023

Chapter 7

Hill, Napoleon. *Think and Grow Rich: The Original, an Official Publication of the Napoleon Hill.* Sound Wisdom (13 December 2016)

Bio

Charlene Harry is a woman who has defied the odds and succeeded in both her personal and professional life. She is happily married with four children, including a rainbow child conceived after forty. Charlene knows what it means to overcome challenges and obstacles. Despite being told that having more children while trying to build a career would negatively impact her career, Charlene went against the odds and became a six-figure earner.

Over a span of 25 years, Charlene moved from level to level working as an engineer in corporate and government roles. She built a diverse skill set that ultimately led her to become a successful business owner. As an author and empowerment speaker, Charlene is passionate about helping overwhelmed and overworked individuals gain clarity on marketing their wisdom to wealth, and helping them reach their full potential.

She is a frequent guest speaker at colleges and corporate events spreading her passion to help students and employees leverage their voice, energize their plan, and capitalize on their talent. Being bold is a great asset when guided by clarity. She helps thousands learn to amplify their inner voice, overcome imposter syndrome as they discover their hidden talents, and use their intellect to gain more.

Charlene is the author of "Stop Settling! *You were Designed for Greatness*," a personal development book that encourages readers to break free from limiting beliefs and unlock their full potential. With her expertise as an alignment coach and transformational career and life consultant, Charlene has helped countless individuals achieve greater clarity and confidence in their personal and professional lives. Her mission is to not only empower but inspire others to create their own success stories and live a life in alignment with the internal voice, full of passion and abundance.

Book Description

Co-Create With Confidence: Leverage Your Voice and Capitalize On Your Talent is the ultimate roadmap for students and individuals that desire greater abundance and fulfillment. In this empowering book, readers will discover practical strategies for identifying and unlocking their unique talents, while learning how to balance work, family, and personal pursuits.

Written specifically for students and employees, this book offers valuable insights and tools to help readers tap into their inner strength and resilience. During the process, you will also explore the spiritual and emotional dimensions of personal growth. From setting clear goals and priorities to managing stress and self-care, *Co-Create with Confidence* provides a comprehensive blueprint for success in every area of life.

With engaging real-life examples and thought-provoking exercises, this book is the perfect guide for any student or professional looking to reclaim their power and transform their life. Whether you're in school, a recent graduate, or on the job as a seasoned executive, this book will help you unlock your full potential and achieve your goals with greater clarity and confidence.

SCAN ME

It's time to start and finish **YOUR Story**!

KLE Publishing specializes in helping people become authors. In as little as 15 to 90 days, we can help you develop your book and publish to 39,000 outlets! Need help with marketing, promotion, building out your coaching or speaking platform, KLE can help make books a part of **YOUR** business!

Ghostwrite, Edit, Format, Publish
We can help from **Start to Finish.**

Finance options available.
No Credit Check or
Minimum Score required
to qualify.*

KLEPub.com Store

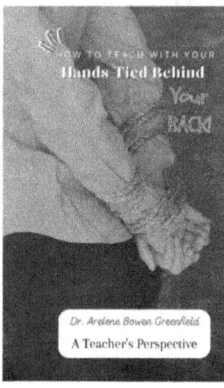